UKLA

The United Kingdom Literacy Association

GW00504268

Creative Planning
with Whole Texts

by Sue McGonigle

Minibook 47

UKLA Minibook Series

Series Editors Penny Manford
Past Editors Rachael Levy, Eve Bearne, Alison B. Littlefair, Bobbie Neate,
Ros Fisher, Susan Ellis

Minibooks in print

**Classroom Action Research in Literacy:
a Guide to Practice** Eve Bearne, Lynda Graham
and Jackie Marsh

**Active encounters: Inspiring young
readers and writers of non-fiction 4-11** Margaret Mallett

Poetry Matters (revised second edition) Andrew Lambirth

**Dyslexia and Inclusion: supporting
classroom reading with 7-11 year olds** Rosemary Anderson

**Practical Bilingual Strategies for
Multilingual Classrooms** Tözün Issa and Alayne Öztürk

**Tell Me Another: Speaking, Listening
and Learning Through Storytelling** Jacqueline Harrett

**Drama: Reading, Writing and
Speaking Our Way Forward** Teresa Grainger and Angela Pickard

**Reading Magazines with a Critical Eye
in the Primary School** Carolyn Swain

Miscue Analysis in the Classroom
(Third Edition) Robin Campbell

The Digital Literacy Classroom Glenn Stone

Making Reading Mean (Revised Edition) Vivienne Smith

Children's Writing Journals
(Revised Edition) Lynda Graham and Annette Johnson

**Literature Circles: Better Talking,
More Ideas** (Second Edition) Carole King and Jane Briggs

Talk for Reading Claire Warner

**Reading motivation and engagement
in the primary school classroom** Sarah P. McGeown

**Storyline: Promoting Language
Across the Curriculum** Steve Bell and Sallie Harkness

Fifty years of literacy education Margaret Cook with Alison Littlefair

**iPads and Tablets in the Classroom:
Personalising children's stories** Natalia Kucirkova

**Evaluating Online Information
and Sources** Andrew K. Shenton and
Alison J. Pickard

Talk for Spelling (Revised Edition) Tony Martin

**Teaching comprehension through
reading and responding to film** Fiona Maine

Film Education, Literacy and Learning Becky Parry with Jeannie Hill Bulman

**Embedding media literacy across
the secondary curriculum** Julian McDougall and Helen Ward

Creative Planning with Whole Texts

Contents

Chapter 1   **Introduction:**
A literature-based approach to planning   1
Rationale   1

Chapter 2   **Choosing texts**   4
Criteria for choosing texts   4
How to 'pitch' books   5
Ensuring a range   5
Implications   11

Chapter 3   **Creative teaching approaches**   12
Reading aloud   12
Booktalk   13
Drama – working in role   15
Visual approaches   17

Chapter 4   **Constructing a teaching sequence**   21
Steps to follow when planning with a text   21
Introducing the text   22
Selecting teaching approaches   22
Outcomes   24
Cross-curricular opportunities   24
A health warning   25
Working with a novel   25

Chapter 5   **A sample teaching sequence**   29
A three week teaching sequence suitable
for children aged 7-9   29

Chapter 6   **Developing writing within a creative**
approach to planning with literature   37
Writing opportunities within a
teaching sequence   37
Creating a sense of purpose and audience   37
Fictional texts as a context for a range of writing   38

continues over

Routines for writing   40

Grammar: writer intention, reader response
and creative imitation   40

Teaching approaches that help in developing
an awareness of writer's use of language   41

Chapter 7   **Conclusion**   43

References: Children's literature   45

Picture books KS1   45

Picture books KS2   45

Novels   46

Traditional stories   47

Non-fiction books   47

Poetry   47

Film   48

Useful links   48

References   49

A digital resource to accompany this Minibook
is available at **http://bit.ly/2BwP6wf**

continues over

List of Figures

3.1 Exploring a text through drama 15

3.2 Chart of creative teaching approaches 19,20

4.1 Planning proforma 23

4.2 Whole class poetry writing in response to
The Wolf Wilder 26

4.3 Art work inspired by *The Wolf Wilder* 27

5.1 Cover illustration *The Bear and the Piano* 29

5.2 Children discuss their responses to an illustration 30

5.3 Illustration from *The Bear and the Piano* 32

5.4 Arranging words and phrases to create a poem 33

5.5 Individual poem inspired by story and illustration in
The Bear and the Piano 34

6.1 A news report inspired by a narrative poem 38

6.2 Text marking: selecting memorable language 41

Acknowledgements

Illustrations from *The Bear and the Piano* © David Litchfield 2015.

My thanks go to:

David Litchfield and Frances Lincoln books for kind permission to use illustrations from *The Bear and the Piano*.

Becky Lawrence, teachers and children of Hill Mead School, Brixton.

Claire Nuttall and staff of St George's International School, Luxembourg.

Ruth Wheatley UCL Institute of Education PGCE student 2016-17.

Nicola Christopher and the Year 6 book group at Princess Frederica C of E Primary school, Brent.

Laura Coyle, Woodlands Primary school, Renfrewshire.

Former colleagues (2004-2013) from whom I learnt so much and in particular Olivia O'Sullivan and Jane Bunting.

Jess Anderson and Frances Bodger for their helpful and astute comments during the development of this minibook. Derek McGonigle for his careful proof reading.

UKLA Minibooks' series editor Penny Manford and Publications Editor Eve Bearne for their advice and guidance.

Chapter 1

Introduction: A literature-based approach to planning

The aim of this Minibook is to provide guidance on how to approach planning around a text in the primary school, with a particular focus on fictional texts. Consideration is given to what to look for when choosing texts, the types of teaching approaches likely to engage children and the linked language and literacy opportunities which can emerge when using these. This approach can excite learners, support teachers in developing their pedagogy and support schools in building an engaging English curriculum with literature at its heart.

Rationale

Carefully chosen literature placed at the centre of the literacy curriculum has the capacity to engage and inspire both children and teachers. It can provide an exciting and inclusive context for a range of speaking, listening, reading and writing activities. By reading books aloud and pausing at key moments to explore stories in depth through talk, drama and arts based approaches, children can become totally immersed in the story world. Through active participation children's enjoyment, understanding and emotional engagement with the experiences of the characters will increase, as this comment from a Year 3 teacher indicates:

> 'It is lovely when they get so caught up with the book. It is real to them. They start thinking like the characters.'

The focus here is on narrative in a variety of forms - picturebooks, novels, traditional story, literary non-fiction and film. Narrative is a fundamental means by which we make sense of our world and our experiences (Hardy, 1977:12) and the 'groundbase' of children's literature in the primary school (Meek Spencer in Barrs and Cork, 2001:15).

The importance of literature goes beyond the benefits for children's language and literacy development. This is acknowledged within The National Curriculum (DfE, 2013:3), which notes the key role reading and literature in particular play in children's development - culturally, emotionally, intellectually, socially and spiritually. Through fiction children can experience books which reflect their own thoughts and feelings or which extend their thinking by introducing new viewpoints (Cremin, 2009:101). Research into cognitive approaches to children's literature indicates that through literature children can develop their theory of mind and empathy as they explore how fictional characters think and feel (Kidd and Costano, 2013; Nikolajeva, 2013). Fictional worlds can provide exciting contexts for a range of purposeful writing and creative work that will not only draw children into a particular book and associated literacy activities, but also help them see the pleasure that books and reading can bring (O'Sullivan and McGonigle, 2010).

It is no surprise that children and young people who read for pleasure score more highly in reading tests. National Literacy Trust research has shown an identifiable link between reading, reading behaviour and attainment (Clark, 2013:20). It has also been shown that 'reading for pleasure', defined by Bearne and Reedy as '[p]ersonal motivation and engagement in reading which leads to sustained voluntary reading' (2018:146), is not only associated with higher reading attainment but also with cognitive success more generally, and that the effect of this continues as children grow up (Sullivan and Brown, 2013). However, the Progress in International Reading Literacy Study (PIRLS) produced every five years has raised concerns about children in England and their attitudes to books and reading. Although the situation is improving, the 2016 PIRLS study still shows that 20% of children in England, more than the international average, report disliking reading (DfE, 2017:102). In terms of attainment, a poverty gap is indicated. The characteristics identified as most strongly predictive of PIRLS performance in 2016 include the number of books the pupil has in their home and their socio-economic status (as determined by historical free-school-meal eligibility) (DfE, 2017:15).

Other studies have indicated that reading engagement is more important than socio-economic background for children's progress as readers (OECD, 2002). As Smith (2016) powerfully points out, children's literature has the potential to close the attainment gap and achieve equity. This has implications not only for resourcing – Smith, for example, suggests 'flooding' nurseries and schools with books and stories - but also for the responsibility of educators to introduce and explore books in the classroom that will challenge and inspire young learners. A 'reimagining' of the English curriculum (Moss, 2017:63) with a central role for literature is an opportunity to address this. The importance of sharing and exploring literature with children should not be underestimated:

> *Children's literature is where children learn to live. It is that important and it deserves a central place in the curriculum.* (Smith, 2016:14)

The following chapters provide a guide to working with literature creatively in the primary classroom. Chapter 3 introduces the types of teaching approaches which might be used to explore texts. Chapter 4 outlines how to go about planning round a complete text, with particular focus on a novel. This process is exemplified further in Chapter 5 which describes a teaching sequence based on a picturebook. Chapter 6 considers developing writing within a text based approach. The first step is to consider how to choose suitable texts. This is the focus of Chapter 2.

Chapter 2

Choosing texts

One of the first considerations when adopting a literature based approach to planning is which texts to use and how to make choices. This chapter addresses these concerns and the implications for teachers.

Careful choice is important if the aim is to engage children, support in-depth exploration and provide the context for a meaningful range of literacy and language activities. It is important to avoid being 'casual' about text choices, literature cannot 'look after itself' (Meek, 1988:6; Smith, 2016:610). If chosen wisely, literature can have the effect of being potentially 'transformational' in terms of children's (and indeed teachers') engagement with books, reading and literacy in general (O'Sullivan and McGonigle, 2010:55).

Criteria for choosing texts

When choosing texts which will lend themselves to being explored in depth in the classroom (sometimes referred to as 'rich texts' (Tennent *et al.*, 2016:23)), considering the following questions may be helpful:

1. Is there a strong narrative and an engaging story?

2. Does the text have engaging illustrations that add to the storytelling and invite response?

3. Are there interesting, appealing or distinctive characters? For example, characters such as Bradley Chambers, the 'bad' boy readers come to know and understand in *There's a Boy in the Girls' Bathroom* by Louis Sachar; or Auggie, the child coping with a facial abnormality in R.J Palacio's *Wonder*. These 'care actors' (characters) can cause readers to want to 'linger' in their worlds a bit longer to reflect on their experiences (Roser *et al.*, 2007:548).

4. Does the text have memorable language? This could be literary language as found in Alfred Noyes' classic poem 'The Highwayman', or language echoing speech patterns as in Libby Hathorn's *Way Home*, a picturebook which tells the story of a child living on the streets.

5. Are there interesting themes which encourage discussion, with relevance to children's lives or that may extend their experience and knowledge of the world?

6. Is this an 'emotionally powerful' text (Barrs and Cork 2001: 215) with which children are likely to make a connection?

7. Does the story make connections with, and build on, children's own experiences and popular culture? Mini Grey's *Traction Man is Here*, written in super hero style, is a popular and successful example of this (O'Sullivan and McGonigle, 2010:56).

Clearly you would not expect to tick all boxes with every text. However, there should be reasons for choosing one book rather than another, reasons which relate to its qualities as a work of literature and its potential for children's engagement and creative exploration in the classroom.

How to 'pitch' books

The books chosen for a literature curriculum are likely to be challenging as independent reads for the majority of the class. For example, the exciting adventure mystery story *Varjak Paw* by S.F. Said, a very popular focus text for lower key stage two, may be challenging as an independent text for Year 3 or 4 readers. Books like this become accessible to children through the teacher reading them aloud, opportunities for talk and the approaches chosen to explore them. The focus is on developing children's response, engagement and comprehension, rather than skills in decoding the text independently.

Ensuring a range

To ensure children have a broad and balanced experience, a range of literature should be provided (Gamble, 2013), including picturebooks, novels, traditional stories from different cultures, myths and legends, poetry, information and also film texts. The variety of character, context and emotion explored within narratives should also be considered (Tennent *et al.*, 2016:33). The aim is to increase children's experience, promote their engagement and provide a rich context for a range of literacy and language work.

While it is important to acknowledge and respond to children's interests and ensure these are represented within classroom collections available for independent reading, it is also important to extend their experience so they have the opportunity to learn about life. The literature which is read aloud to children or chosen to focus on and explore over time has the potential to do this.

Picturebooks

Picturebooks have an important role within a literature programme for children throughout primary school. They can provide an exciting and inclusive context for learning, beneficial to all children, including those who find literacy challenging and children with English as an additional language (EAL) (Arizpe and Styles 2015:180).

In the best contemporary picturebooks, word and image interact to tell stories which can captivate and challenge. The detailed artwork does much more than merely illustrate the words; it contributes to and extends the narrative, providing much to discover on each re-reading. Well-known examples include Anthony Browne's surreal narratives, such as *Gorilla* or *The Tunnel*. Another very popular picturebook with younger children is Simon Bartram's *Man on the Moon, a day in the life of Bob*. This tells the story of a seemingly ordinary individual with an extraordinary job - he is an astronaut working on the moon. The text repeats Bob's denial that there are aliens on the moon, yet young readers can spot them in nearly every one of the colourful and detailed spreads.

There are increasing numbers of wordless picturebooks which communicate powerful stories through illustration alone. David Wiesner's work, including the mysterious *Tuesday* describing strange night time happenings, is well known. A recent example is *Professional Crocodile* by Zoboli and Di Giorgio, an engaging and amusing narrative with a clever ending which challenges attitudes to wild animals and keeping them in captivity (a theme also developed through words and pictures in Anthony Browne's *Zoo*). Arizpe and Styles (2014) describe the impact on children newly arrived in the UK of collaborative readings and dialogue about a wordless narrative and the exciting writing opportunities which emerged in their work with Shaun Tan's masterpiece, *The Arrival*.

Picturebooks can introduce important themes and feelings in a powerful way. For example, in Benji Davies' *The Storm Whale* the themes of loneliness and responsibility are explored and Oliver Jeffers' *Lost and Found* looks at the power of friendship. Through Ed Vere's *Mr Big*, a story about a lonely gorilla and David Litchfield's *Grandad's Secret Giant*, who dares appear only at night, young children can explore what it might mean to feel different and feared because of it. In addition to these books suitable for younger children, there are many highly sophisticated picturebook narratives with themes which can challenge older readers and provide a vehicle to discuss controversial issues, as is demonstrated by Janet Evans' research (2015). *The Island* by Armin Greder is one of the books Evans cites. It starkly and shockingly tells a tale of prejudice, fear and cruelty. Another example is *The Promise* by Nicola Davies and Laura Carlin which introduces ideas of regeneration and recompense. Although it may be argued that exploring themes such as these is an opportunity much literature offers, picturebooks have a particular role to play through powerful Illustrations which can express emotion in a way which is easy for young children to 'read' (Nikolajeva, 2013:249).

Novels

In KS2 novels or 'sustained fictional narratives' long enough for detailed development of character and plot (Mallett, 2016:199) will form an important part of a literature programme, both as a serialised class story and as a focus text for exploration during English sessions. Working with a novel presents particular challenges as they are likely to be longer than many picturebooks or traditional stories. These challenges will be addressed further in Chapter 4.

Novels chosen should reflect the best of contemporary literature but may also include modern classics such as *Charlotte's Web* by E.B. White, *The Iron Man* by Ted Hughes and, more recently, David Almond's *Skellig*. There is an increasing number of illustrated novels which merit inclusion, for example *Pugs of the Frozen North* by Philip Reeve and Sarah McIntyre or *The Savage* by David Almond and Dave McKean. A varied experience is important and the chosen texts need to represent a range of genres too. Here is an indication of this with a few examples:

Adventure and mystery

Katherine Rundell's *The Explorer* set in the Amazonian rainforest, takes readers on an exciting adventure in an unfamiliar setting. M.G. Leonard's *Beetle Boy* and Siobhan Dowd's *The London Eye Mystery* involve mysterious disappearances which children will find engrossing and enjoy trying to solve.

Sci-fi and fantasy

Examples include S.F. Said's *Phoenix*, an exciting intergalactic space quest which explores themes of identity and belonging; Abi Elphinstone's *Sky Song* set in the bewitched world of Erkenwald; and the classic adventure in five nights by Ted Hughes about a mysterious Iron Man at first distrusted then called upon to save the world from a greater threat.

Historical novels

Writers such as Berlie Doherty bring the past to life, for example her novel *Treason* is set in London during the reign of Henry VIII. There are a number of engaging children's books set in the Second World War, including Emma Carroll's *Letters to the Lighthouse* and Michelle Magorian's *Goodnight Mister Tom*.

Social Realism

Books with a real life context can expand children's experiences of the situations others face or possibly help them realise that the problems they face themselves are not unique. For example, *Little Bits of Sky* by S.E. Durrant, set in the more recent past, is a moving story about children in care.

Through books such as *Welcome to Nowhere*, set in the contemporary context of the Syrian civil war by Elizabeth Laird, children can begin to understand the plight of refugees.

Traditional stories

Traditional stories, from a range of cultures, represent an important part of any literature programme. Through traditional stories children will enrich their understanding of their own culture and that of others, within their own school, local community and beyond. Within traditional stories there are easily recognisable characters who are good, evil, magic or comic and common themes of greed, jealousy, self-sacrifice or bravery. They have clearly defined narrative structures, frequently featuring repetition in the story line and the language, and often containing a refrain or chorus which is repeated throughout. These features make traditional stories highly memorable, supporting children's oral and written retelling and their understanding of story in general.

Traditional tales will include folk and fairy tales, fables and also myths and legends. Many writers of traditional tales are experienced storytellers themselves, such as Kevin Crossley Holland who has produced beautiful versions of Norse myths and British folk tales. Geraldine McCaughrean, Hugh Lupton and Daniel Morden have produced excellent retellings of the dramatic and heroic tales from Ancient Greece. Chitra Soundar collects and relates stories from India such as the picturebook *Pattan's Pumpkin*, an Indian flood story beautifully illustrated by Frané Lessac. Jessica Souhami's picturebooks include stories from around the world, such as *The Leopard's Drum* from West Africa. *A Year Full of Stories* with 52 folk tales from around the world written by Angela McAllister is a useful resource, providing a good starting point for creative retelling.

Poetry

Poetry is an important area to include in a literature programme. However, choosing and working with poetry is often the area with which teachers feel least confident and knowledgeable (Collins in Cremin *et al.*, 2014.). Narrative poetry can be a great starting point for those unsure about working with poetry. Well known narrative poems include *The Owl and the Pussycat* by Edward Lear, Alfred Noyes *The Highwayman*, Charles Causley's *What has happened to Lulu?* and Ian Seraillier's amusing mystery, *The Visitor*. John Agard's *Windrush Child* about the journey of the first immigrants to Britain from the Caribbean is another example of a poem with a story at its heart. Anthologies can be invaluable resources, when looking for poems of a particular type, or on a particular theme. Several of these are in the list of children's literature references. There are also a number of useful poetry websites including The Poetry Archive http://bit.ly/2G7pvK3 and Poetryline http://bit.ly/2szwada.

Film texts

It is important that a literature curriculum for the 21st century includes audio-visual (film) texts. The role of film in the English curriculum used to be restricted to a supporting role alongside a written text, for example to speed up covering a longer novel by viewing instead of reading some sections, or to compare the openings of film and print versions of the same story. The potential of film is now recognised by educators, in particular through the work of the British Film Institute Education team (BfI) and there is recognition that film merits inclusion as a stand-alone text. This will build on children's home experience of film as an important story telling medium that has a 'fundamental' role in the lives of children of the digital age (Marsh, 2004:35; Parry and Hill Bulman, 2017).

Although popular full feature films such as *Toy Story* might be explored during English sessions, there is also great potential in the use of short films such as *Baboon on the Moon* (Duriez, 2002), an appealing story about a lonely baboon working on the moon, or *The Windmill Farmer* (Baldwin, 2010) which imagines a world in which wind farms are tended by farmers struggling with the elements. Both of these are available via YouTube or Vimeo. With compact narratives, often under ten minutes long, it is possible to view them more than once over a series of sessions or even within a session.

Focus on a film narrative does not only develop children's understanding and response to story, setting or character (conventional literacy skills), but also develops their film literacy knowledge and skills concerning the ways sound, colour and camera are used to tell the story and create effects on the viewer. The Literacy Shed is a very useful curated resource with many short films including the two mentioned above.

Non-fiction texts

Throughout primary school children should experience a range of information books, newspapers and online texts on different topics and in different formats. Many of these will be included in classroom library collections and may be a focus linked to class topics.

In terms of creative exploration through a teaching sequence, the kinds of books which most readily lend themselves to exploration in this way are non-fiction books with a clear narrative, described by Smith (2014:16) as 'literary nonfiction' - a genre of writing telling a factually accurate story, using literary styles and techniques. Examples of these are biographies, such as *Long Walk to Freedom*, Chris Van Wyk's adaptation of Nelson Mandela's life story or Floella Benjamin's autobiography *Coming to England*. Stories of particular events can also be explored through a teaching sequence, for example *The Great Fire of London* (Emma Adams and James Weston Lewis) or *Shackleton's Journey* (William Grill), which tells the Antarctic explorer's story in graphic novel form. Marc Martin's beautiful picturebook telling the story of *A River* invites storytelling, poetry, dance or drama as creative responses to its stunning illustrations.

Implications

Careful choice is important in order to provide quality texts with the emotional power to engage and inspire children (O'Sullivan and McGonigle, 2010). The obvious implication is the need to have a broad knowledge of children's literature. This knowledge needs to be kept up to date, to avoid the dangers of using the same books every year or not considering alternatives, which can lead to a lack of freshness and vitality and many wonderful books being ignored. Research has shown the impact a limited knowledge of children's literature can have on the books teachers introduce in the classroom (O'Sullivan and McGonigle, 2010: 53; Cremin *et al.*, 2014: 49). Although classic literature, including well known picturebooks such as Eric Carle's *The Very Hungry Caterpillar* or novels such as *Charlotte's Web* by EB White, should continue to feature, it is also important to draw on the wealth of contemporary literature which may have additional relevance for children's lives. This requires conscious effort but is well worth it, both for children's engagement and for teachers' satisfaction and enthusiasm. In addition, in order to plan effectively, time needs to be spent getting to know a book, considering its potential and how it might be explored. As Tennent *et al.* (2016:22) suggest '[t]here is no short cut to teaching reading well; you have to know the texts you are using'.

Providing a broad experience at the heart of the curriculum also has an impact on children's knowledge about books and writers (Powell in Cremin *et al.*, 2014:46) and provides a model for how to be a 'discerning reader', able to find and appreciate quality texts (Tennent *et al.*, 2016:33).

Hot seating, whereby children ask questions of one child in role as a character, makes it possible to explore a character's motivation or gaps in the narrative and has the potential to build an imaginative back story. For example: Why did Lulu, in Charles Causley's poem 'What has happened to Lulu?', leave home so mysteriously?

Conscience alley is a means of exploring a character's thoughts and feelings when presented with a dilemma and investigating the complexity of the decision they are facing. The class create two lines facing each other. One child in role as a particular character walks down the 'alley' and listens to children voicing arguments for and against a particular decision or action that the character is facing at a key point in the narrative (DfES 2003). For example: *What should the farmers do about the Iron Man?* or *Should Varjak Paw leave his home and risk the dangers of the city to find help for his family?*

Writing in role following on from, or during drama linked to a text, enables children's imaginative ideas and language to 'percolate' (Grainger *et al.*, 2005:106). Inexperienced writers are supported to move out of their own language register to the language of the text or character, as they 'live' through events in the story (Barrs, 2000:57). Writing in role might be repeated several times within a teaching sequence, perhaps through the vehicle of a character's diary, showing how the events of the story affect a central character and how they respond.

For more on developing writing within a book based approach see Chapter 6.

Visual approaches

Visual approaches can take a variety of forms and not only apply to picture-books but also to texts which are not illustrated.

Responding to illustration

When working with a picturebook, time should be spent looking closely at individual illustrations, exploring them as visual texts. Children should be encouraged to read the images, observe details, make inferences, discuss and note what they see. The teaching sequence in Chapter 5 provides examples of this approach. With wordless narratives children might read the illustrations together and tell the story collaboratively. 'Image-based strategies' such as these (Arizpe and Styles, 2014:212), with an emphasis on talk and the opportunity to use home languages, can be highly accessible ways into literature for children new to English, as Arizpe and Styles' work with David Wiesner's *Flotsam* and Shaun Tan's *The Arrival* illustrates.

Visualisation

When reading as adults we use our knowledge and experience to visualise a scene, setting or character. This is an important skill for children to acquire, enabling them to develop their concept of a storyworld. Children can be asked to think about and discuss what they see or imagine in their mind's eye when listening to descriptive passages of settings or characters in longer narrative texts such as the opening scene of *Phoenix* where stars are described as 'a million points of silver light, shining in the black' (Said, 2013:1) or those describing one of its main characters, Bixa Quicksilver, as 'an alien warrior with neon needles in her hair'. This process will require children to focus closely on the text, articulate their ideas and develop them in response to others.

Drawing

Drawing is a useful thinking tool when exploring texts. Linked to visualisation of a narrative, it can support (and demonstrate) children's understanding of character or place and help them develop ideas for writing as well (O'Sullivan and McGonigle, 2010:57).

Drawing a map can help children develop a concept of the geography of the storyworld, key places where the main events in a story take place, or a character's journey. Sketching a storyboard of the main 'scenes' can support children's understanding of a story's structure and help them with oral or written retelling.

In addition, art work can offer an opportunity for expressive response to literary language and the images evoked, as, for example, those evoked by the opening of Alfred Noyes' poem 'The Highwayman' where 'the road was a ribbon of moonlight over the purple moor.'

The chart which follows contains a longer list of 'tried and tested' teaching approaches. It is not an exhaustive list, but provides a useful guide when planning. The list of approaches should be used selectively - it is not intended that all approaches will be used with every text, but rather that teachers will choose the approaches which they feel are most appropriate to the text they are exploring and the outcomes they are planning. Chapter 5 illustrates this in the context of a teaching sequence. Over the course of a year a range of approaches should be used to provide a broad experience and ensure sessions are varied and engaging.

Creative teaching approaches	Purpose
Teacher reading aloud Teacher reads book aloud, children are active listeners. Requires one copy of text only. If a picture book this should be visible to children.	To engage children with story, 'lift' words off the page and enable all children to have access. Supports children's comprehension through teacher's reading aloud.
Talk based approaches **1.'Booktalk'** sharing responses. Teacher invites dialogue and takes part in exploratory talk as reader her/himself.	To encourage children to develop and articulate their response to a text and begin to consider what it was about a text which created a particular effect/response. A key prerequisite for developing children's comprehension.
2. Storytelling, retelling Teacher tells story. Children retell. **Story Whoosh-** Teacher narrates story inviting children to enter the story circle and re-enact parts of text. On teacher's 'whoosh' children return to their place.	To develop understanding of narrative structure and experience of literary language. Supports narrative writing. Story whoosh provides overview.
3. Oral performance – readers' theatre and poetry performance A 'script' is prepared from a text collaboratively, rehearsed and performed	To engage children, enable them to become more aware of literary language and savour it, allowing for creative and playful interpretation. Supports comprehension.
4. Debate e.g. What should be done with the Iron man? (Hughes, 1968) Should Fred keep the Explorer's secret? (Rundell, 2017)	Oral rehearsal for preparation for written arguments. Supports understanding of dilemma and viewpoint.
5. Drama, working in role: *Role play, thought tracking and hot seating* (i.e. one individual in role as fictional character is questioned by class).	To enable children to 'step inside a story' and explore it from a character's perspective, explore dilemma and motivation.

continues over

This might include teacher in role, particularly if children are less experienced with working in role. *Conscience alley:* What should a character do at this point in the story? Child in role walks through 'alley' of children who offer different advice. Re-enactment through small world play or story themed role play areas.	Develops empathy. Important preparation for writing in role as a character.
Other approaches **Visual approaches** Respond to an illustration e.g. what do you see/think/wonder? Visualisation and drawing of a scene or character. Storyboarding of the key scenes in a narrative or mapping of the geography of a story or a character's journey.	Responding to illustration helps to deepen engagement, prediction, inference and deduction and is inclusive. Visualisation and drawing develop and demonstrate inference and deduction. Storyboarding and mapping helps plot and sequence key events in a narrative; supports narrative retelling and narrative writing.
Soundscape Inspired by a story. Created using voice/body percussion/percussion instruments/selected soundclips.	To support imaginative engagement, creative response and build a sense of time and place.
Dance and music Expressive response to a text through dance to teacher-selected music or creating own music in response to a text.	To provide opportunities for creative interpretation of a text.
Text marking Children select key parts of a text which are memorable to them.	Focus on literary language and meaning. Class and individual collections can be made which children can use in their own writing.
Film literacy techniques Looking at use of sound, camera angle/shot, colour/light.	For exploring film texts in addition to other approaches. To see how filmic devices help tell a story.

Figure 3.2: Chart of creative teaching approaches

Chapter 4

Constructing a teaching sequence

This chapter describes how to go about constructing a teaching sequence around a text. Some key steps for successful planning are included. A framework for planning is provided (Figure 4.1). This may prove helpful when considering the strengths of a book or other text, key points to pause and explore, appropriate teaching approaches and possible outcomes. The implications of working with longer narratives are explored and key points to note when looking for opportunities to making cross curricular links are identified. After consideration of these a session by session sequence can be created. To illustrate this, a sample teaching sequence based on a rich picturebook is included in Chapter 5.

Steps to follow when planning with a text

Step one	Choose a text which will support exploration over time. These are frequently referred to as 'rich' or 'quality' texts. *See Chapter 2 for guidance on choosing texts and the range children should experience.*
Step two	Read the text yourself carefully. Respond initially as a reader: what do you like about this text? Consider what its key features and strengths are: these are what you will want to highlight in the teaching sequence you create.
Step three	Consider key moments in the narrative to pause and explore, for example if a character faces a dilemma or needs to make a decision.
Step four	Choose the most appropriate teaching approaches to highlight key aspects of the text and to explore key moments in the narrative. *See Chapter 3 for information on a range of teaching approaches and their purpose.*

Step five	Consider the range of writing opportunities or other outcomes which might seem appropriate. These might include performance or multi-media outcomes.
Step six	Consider meaningful or relevant cross curricular links; opportunities for creative expression through arts based subjects; and the text's potential for children's personal development, their sense of self and ability to empathise.

Introducing the text

There are a number of ways to introduce a text. Traditionally this has been to look at the cover together, considering the title and illustration and inviting speculation about the story before beginning to read it aloud. Although perfectly valid, it is worth considering other approaches. For example, with a picturebook, revealing one illustration from within a story and inviting discussion around that can be an engaging way in (as illustrated in Chapter 5). A novel might be introduced by simply reading the opening aloud before the title is known or the cover seen. Alternatively, to introduce a book with a less familiar setting, images of the landscape might be displayed or artefacts related to a story produced to encourage speculation. Publishers are increasingly producing book trailers which are an exciting way to whet children's appetites before beginning to read a book aloud. (See for example the trailer for S.F. Said's sci-fi adventure *Phoenix* https://www.youtube.com/watch?v=p5yQjwqDFXA .)

Selecting teaching approaches

Although the teacher reading aloud or storytelling, talk and drama will be key teaching approaches to draw on (as mentioned in Chapter 3), it is not necessary, or advisable, to plan to use every teaching approach suggested in Figure 3.2 with every text. Teaching approaches should be chosen according to the type of text, its particular strengths, the aims for children's learning and the intended outcomes.

Certain types of text may suggest particular approaches. For example, when working with picturebooks responding to the illustrations is important whereas traditional stories lend themselves to storytelling.

Planning creatively around a text

Text:

Author/illustrator:

Strengths:

Themes:

How to introduce the book and points to pause	Teaching approaches and aims	Writing or other outcomes	Cross-curricular and IPC links

Resources including related books and poems

Outcomes

When planning around a text it is important to consider carefully the types of outcomes which might emerge. In many cases these are likely to be pieces of writing, for example a retelling of a story from a different perspective or a newspaper report of a dramatic section of a story. The teaching sequence in Chapter 5 indicates how writing can form the outcome of a sequence of activities and approaches. However outcomes might not all be written, for example a final outcome could be a film, or perhaps a news broadcast with reports of key events and interviews with the main characters. In this case, the writing children do will be in preparation for the news broadcast itself.

Cross-curricular opportunities

Children's literature can provide an exciting context for learning with meaningful links to be made across the curriculum. In addition, rich texts will provide opportunities for creative expression through arts based subjects and many will offer potential for children's personal and emotional development and understanding of the world.

Science and Humanities

A Science topic on Space would be significantly enhanced with a focus on *A Day in the Life of Bob, Man on the Moon* by Simon Bartram with younger children or S.F. Said's intergalactic adventure *Phoenix* with older children.

Historical topics such as the Victorians and Britain at War can be brought to life through stories such as Berlie Doherty's *Street Child* or Emma Carroll's *Letters to the Lighthouse*. A geographical sense of place can be built through story, for example *The Explorer* by Katherine Rundell enables children to step into the Amazonian rainforest.

PSHE, knowledge of the world and environmental awareness

There are many wonderful books which merit exploration but may not have obvious links across the primary curriculum. Often they include themes which support children's personal development and understanding of the world. *The Bear and the Piano*, introduced in Chapter 5, is an example of this. The picturebook *On Sudden Hill* by Linda Sarah and Benji Davies explores the changing dynamics of friendship. Graeme Baker Smith's picturebook *FArTHER* looks at the father son relationship, love and loss.

Left: Figure 4.1 Planning proforma

Environmental awareness can be developed through a sequence based on *Tidy* by Emily Gravett, *Pandora* by Victoria Turnbull or *The Promise* by Nicola Davies and Laura Carlin. Awareness of the plight of endangered animals and natural resources could be considered through the novels of Gill Lewis including *Skyhawk* and *Gorilla Dawn*.

The refugee experience can be made comprehensible for children with books such as *My name is not Refugee* by Kate Milner, *Welcome to Nowhere* by Elizabeth Laird and *The Journey* by Francesca Sanna.

Creative arts

Exploring a rich text provides opportunity for children to respond in a variety of ways, not only through writing but also through the creative arts, for example producing art work, music or dance inspired by the snowy landscapes of Rundell's *The Wolf Wilder* (as described below). Study of *The Iron Man* is likely to lead naturally to making junk models of the Iron Man.

A health warning

It is very easy, with a busy curriculum, to choose focus books solely because they 'fit' with a particular topic. This can lead to children's literature being viewed as purely functional, at the service of the broader curriculum. Book choice may be compromised by this approach, meaning texts chosen might not be as strong and therefore less likely to engage children or merit in-depth exploration. It can also lead to wonderful books, which could provide a rich and memorable literary experience for children, being ignored.

Working with a novel

Novels, which are likely to form an important part of a literature curriculum for children in KS2, present particular challenges when constructing a teaching sequence because of the length of the text. In order to plan a sequence of about four weeks, allow time to get to know the story really well yourself and give careful thought to its strengths, choosing key points to pause and explore. This may be, for example, when a character has to make a choice or faces a dilemma. It is not be possible to explore every aspect of the plot, or perhaps every chapter of a longer book. The central teaching approach is reading the whole text aloud. Opportunities need to be found for this at separate times in the school day, so that particular points in the narrative can be reached and explored during English lessons.

To illustrate this an exemplar four week teaching sequence for the novel *The Wolf Wilder* by Katherine Rundell, suitable for ages 9-11, can be found here **http://bit.ly/2BwP6wf** .

An exciting adventure story, *The Wolf Wilder* is set in pre-revolutionary Russia. This is a novel with clearly drawn characters, memorable scenes, striking language and a satisfying storyline. There are strong themes running through the story, including bravery and its many forms. Beautifully written, this novel is a delight to read aloud and has lots to offer in terms of creative exploration in the Primary classroom. It can inspire a range of writing. The suggested teaching sequence referred to above includes narrative, instructional and persuasive writing, and poetry. Figure 4.2 illustrates a wonderful example of a whole class poem written in response to the story

---

The Soldiers are near...

The cold wind whistling an icy tune
As the wolves are grizzly growling
Coldness rubbing against skin making it tingle
As a fire is sparking close by

The wind screaming in fear
The soldiers may be near...

A dark frosty forest lit up with sparkling snow
Far off shouting in the distance
Wolves' teeth chattering in the cold

The wind screaming in fear
The soldiers may be near...

Muffled growling as wolves softly dream
under the rustling trees
Rakov's cold heart lurking in the shadows
Waiting to pounce

The wind screaming in fear
The soldiers may be near...

The branches shaking wildly
Under the weight of snow
Wolves quietly purring
In their comfortable sleep

The wind screaming in fear
The soldiers may be near...

Freezing sharp wind stabbing at the trees
Bitter, icy, cold
Wolves snoring, scratching, snuffling
Whilst birds speak noisily above

The wind screaming in fear
The soldiers may be near...

Snow landing softly like a fluffy pillow
Peaceful yet scary
Little Lapushka and her cubs trembling in the woods
Faint screams rise from a village close by

The wind screaming in fear
The soldiers are getting near...

The Imperials searching the forest
Like predators hunting their prey.
Loud feet crunching through the deep white snow
The pack in panic and shock and fear

The soldiers are definitely near...

The trees rustling intensely
the wind vibrating like hearts filled with fear

The soldiers are actually here...

Figure 4.2: Whole class poetry in response to The Wolf Wilder

and its illustrations. Writing in role is repeated at different points in the sequence to explore the main character's changing thoughts and feelings. See Chapter 6 for more detail on writing within a book based approach and Chapter 3 for more on writing in role as a teaching approach.

A range of drama approaches such as freeze frame, hot seating and role play are suggested to explore significant events in the story and understand how the main characters respond to their situations. Other key approaches include visualising the vividly described settings and characters, considering how the writer has used language to create particular effects, and responding to descriptions of the wolves through art work as illustrated in Figure 4.3.

Figure 4.3:
Art work inspired
by The Wolf Wilder

A class debate is suggested to explore a particular point in the narrative and booktalk opportunities are incorporated throughout the sequence to discuss important themes and consider children's thoughts and feelings about the characters:

> *"My favourite character was Feo - I really loved how she was so kind to the wolves, how she welcomed them, most people would be frightened and scared of wolves, she was really powerful."* (Year 6 girl, Brent)

"And she was brave - about her mum being gone." (Year 6 boy, Brent)

The richness of this text supports in-depth exploration as Laura, a teacher from Renfrewshire comments:

> *"The Wolf Wilder gives lots of areas to focus on as a class novel. Not just the themes: friendships, survival and many more but also the language. Having great illustrations to accompany the text really helps too. This book is challenging but with a teacher guided approach I really saw some children begin to form a love of reading through this book."*

In terms of resourcing, class sets of novels are not necessary. One copy is all you need to read the book aloud. However. a small set can be useful, for example if you decide to return to a particular passage with a small group. If available in the class library collection, these extra copies are likely to be in demand once you have finished the story. It is useful to have a class reading journal when exploring a novel. This could take the form of an A3 book to gather comments about the book as a whole, the characters, plot or language.

When beginning to plan around a text for the first time a picturebook, or other shorter text such as a traditional story may be a less daunting choice. The following chapter includes an exemplar teaching sequence based on a picturebook suitable for children aged 7-9. The approaches suggested can be applied or adapted for use with other picturebooks and for older or younger children.

Chapter 5

A sample teaching sequence

This chapter presents a sample teaching sequence based on *The Bear and the Piano* by David Litchfield (Frances Lincoln). The approach illustrated is of a text being gradually unfolded, 'a slow reveal' as one Year 4 teacher described it. This is an approach which has been found to really engage children. They are eager to find out what happens next as they become more immersed in the story world (O'Sullivan and McGonigle, 2010).

There is an emphasis on reading aloud, talk and drama-based approaches. These approaches are intended to be inclusive, however there is a need to consider the needs of individuals and groups of children within the class when preparing short term planning. Sessions are approximately an hour in length. The session overview is an indication only and additional time may be needed for some of the activities, in particular written tasks. Chapter 6 provides greater detail about writing within a literature programme.

Figure 5.1: Cover illustration from The Bear and the Piano

A three week teaching sequence suitable for children aged 7-9

This sequence provides an opportunity to explore a range of National Curriculum objectives for English, in particular the Lower Key Stage Two statutory requirements for comprehension including:

- asking questions to improve understanding of the text;
- inferring characters' feelings thoughts and motives;
- participating in discussion about books which are read to them.

(DfE, 2013:26)

A brief synopsis of the story

One day a young bear cub finds a piano in the forest. He has never seen one before and doesn't know what it is or does. Gradually he finds out

Figure 5.5: Individual poem inspired by story and illustration in The Bear and the Piano

Session eight: **Writing in role**

In this session children consider the bear's feelings at this point in the story and express these through diary writing in role.

Read aloud the text on the double page with the illustration of the bear on the rooftops. Ask children to write in role as if in the bear's diary that night.

Session nine: **Draw the next scene**

In this session, rather than asking children to predict what will happen next, they are asked what their preferred outcome is i.e. a 'reader question' rather than a 'text question' (Martin, 2011:40).

As a class, review what has just happened in the story then ask the children:

What would you like to happen next?

What would you choose as the next scene in the story?

Ask children to illustrate their chosen next scene. Share children's imaginary scenes and discuss why they chose to portray a particular scene.

Session ten: **Sharing responses**

In this session children listen to the remainder of the story, reflect on the book as a whole and share their responses to it.

Read on to the end of the story. Encourage the class to share their responses to the story as a whole:

What did you like about the book? Was there anything you disliked?

What would you tell someone else about this story?

If given the opportunity for this kind of dialogue, children's comments can demonstrate they are reflective and perceptive, as the following comments from two eight year old girls in Bethnal Green, London indicate:

'It teaches you to never give up. The bear never gives up, he plays for days and weeks and months and years until he is ready.'

'It's a nice story because even though the bear went to the city, the others were happy for him.'

Sessions 11: Hot seating

In this session children have the opportunity to think more deeply and imaginatively about the bear's experience and the feelings of his friends in the forest. Before this session find time to re-read the whole story aloud.

As a class, discuss the questions other bears in the forest might ask the main character about his experience. Working with a partner, ask children to try out some questions they might ask and think about how the bear might answer. Follow this with a whole class hot seating activity, with one child in role as the bear and the rest of the class asking questions as if they are one of the bears in the forest. If children are less confident with hot seating you could take the role of the bear yourself.

Session 12: Story mapping and 'storytelling'

This session provides an overview of the key events in the story and an opportunity to rehearse retelling orally before writing individually.

As a class, discuss the key events in *The Bear and the Piano*. Note these on a flip chart or board. After this, ask children to work with a partner and construct a storyboard of the main events in the story.

Gather the class in a large space such as a hall and seat children in a circle. Begin a retelling of story of the *Bear and the Piano* as if from the bear's perspective. Invite individuals to continue the story in role. Children then work with a partner to retell their own version from the bear's point of view, using their storyboards and their own ideas.

Session 13 and 14: **Narrative writing in role as the bear. Shared and individual writing**

Two sessions which lead to the final piece of writing - a retelling of the story in first person as the bear.

As a shared writing activity, demonstrate how a narrative written from the bear's point of view might begin. Children continue the story either using this beginning, or writing their own. After drafting their stories, children could work with a partner to edit them before rewriting in mini books and adding their own illustrations. The finished books could be displayed in the classroom or elsewhere in the school.

The approaches used in this teaching sequence can be adapted for other picturebooks and for older or younger children. For a selection of other exemplar teaching sequences based on quality texts see here **http://bit.ly/2BwP6wf**.

Chapter 6

Developing writing within a creative approach to planning with literature

Literature offers a range of possibilities for writers… at times this will be imitative, but at others literature will be engaged with as a source of inspiration and ideas. (Cremin, 2009:108)

A fictional text can provide an exciting context for a range of writing opportunities. Research has shown that working in depth with carefully chosen literature has huge potential, not only in terms of children's engagement and progress in reading but also for their writing (O'Sullivan and McGonigle, 2010; Barrs, 2000). Time spent 'dwelling on texts' (Barrs, 2000:59), reading them aloud, discussing them and exploring them through a range of approaches is very important.

Writing opportunities within a teaching sequence

Working in this way is more fluid than a 'big write' once a week approach. Writing activities are built in as appropriate to the unfolding story and after experiences which provide suitable preparation. The sample sequence for *The Bear and the Piano* has illustrated how to include a variety both of short pieces of writing: to a fictional character, poetry, and writing in role; and two longer pieces: the news report and narrative writing in role. The experience of hearing the story read aloud, discussing and responding to the story and illustrations and stepping into the narrative through drama and role play are essential preparation for children's writing. This creative immersion in the text is crucial in supporting children in both having something they want to write, and rehearsing the language with which to say it.

Creating a sense of purpose and audience

It is well recognised that children are more motivated to write if they have a sense of purpose and audience (DfE, 2008; DfE, 2012). Sometimes this might be a real life context, for example writing to the head teacher about permission to play football at playtimes. However, once immersed in the world of a story, literature can offer a gripping context and purpose for writing too. Although fictional, this will feel real to children who are caught up in an exciting narrative. Children care about what happens to characters they feel they have come to know and are eager to write to them, perhaps with advice when they face a dilemma. Through drama, they are able to step into a character's shoes and are keen to write in role. With in-depth knowledge of the story and experience of being the character, *what* to write is not a problem.

There are a number of ways an audience for writing can be created so that children do not feel they write "for my teacher to see how good you are" as one Year 5 boy once told me (McGonigle, 2002:62). These include writing for publication on a school website and creating class or individual books, for example to represent a character's diary. At times the purpose for writing can be to prepare for another 'outcome', for example storytelling, poetry performance, PowerPoint presentation or news broadcast as suggested in Chapter 4.

Fictional texts as a context for a range of writing

It may be feared that working from a narrative text might mean that any writing produced will be narrative as well. In fact, a carefully chosen text can lead to a range of writing in different genres.

Figure 6.1: A news report inspired by a narrative poem

Newspaper reports built around an unfolding narrative often work well, as in the sequence on *The Bear and the Piano* in the previous chapter or the example illustrated in Figure 6.1 This news report, the work of a Year 6 child in Luxembourg, was written in response to Ian Seraillier's narrative poem 'The Visitor' which tells the eerie but amusing story of a man who steals a ring from a skeleton in a churchyard and is then pursued by the skeleton when he returns home with it. A teaching sequence based on this poem is available at **http://bit.ly/2BwP6wf**. Other writing opportunities linked to this poem include interviews and narrative writing from different viewpoints.

A non-fiction writing focus might follow or precede a teaching sequence based on a narrative. For example, *Beetle Boy* by M.G. Leonard may lead to interest in beetles and stimulate research and non-chronological report writing on the subject. Similarly with younger children, *Superbat* by Matt Carr may lead to interest and research into bats. A focus on hunter gatherers might precede a sequence on *Wolf Brother*, Michelle Paver's exciting adventure quest story set 6000 years ago, to develop a sense of historical context (Bunting *et al.*, 2011:58).

Through one text, children could potentially experience a range of writing genres. For example, the novel *Wolf Brother* can lend itself to report writing about wolves or hunter gatherers, or discursive writing about the merits of a wolf cub as a guide, as well as narrative writing and poetry. If children are unfamiliar with a particular genre, it is helpful to read an example aloud so that they hear how the written language sounds, or to display an example so that a typical layout is visible and aspects of style and structure can be highlighted. It may be that shared writing to 'tune children in' to a less familiar type of writing is sufficient. There is a need to be sensitive to this. An over-analytical approach can disrupt a teaching sequence and have a negative effect on children's engagement with the story, a particular activity or even with writing in general.

For schools adopting a book-based approach more widely, different types of writing will be revisited over the course of a year, as appropriate in response to a particular text. If over time teachers feel there are gaps in the range children are experiencing, this could be addressed through additional writing tasks linked to a particular book, where this seems appropriate, or through writing linked to other curriculum areas or school events.

Stimulating children to write through creative approaches with engaging literature can inspire young writers and is likely to lead to more varied language use and sentence structures, 'echoing' a focus text (Barrs, 2001: 203). For example, the novel *Wolf Brother* includes this prophecy:

> *Deepest of all the drowned sight*
> *Oldest of all the stone bite*
> *Coldest of all the darkest light* (Paver, 2004:102)

Children can tune into the style and use the cadences in their own writing as this example from a child in Year 6 in North Somerset illustrates:

'And speaking with silence,
Don't make a sound,
This is the prophecy that we speak,
That people find and seek.' (Bunting *et al.*, 2011: 61)

However, providing inspiration and a sense of purpose is not enough in itself for children to make progress in all aspects of writing. Teachers also need to ensure routines are in place so that children can develop their skills.

Routines for writing

Routines include time for preparation, demonstration and scaffolding through modelled and shared writing, guided group work and collaborative writing. Time also needs to be allowed for developing and reviewing writing. Building in reasons for redrafting for some pieces of work (perhaps for publication on a school website or bookmaking) will encourage closer attention to vocabulary choices and transcriptional matters of punctuation, spelling and presentation. Teachers may find there is a need to build in additional time to develop writing within a teaching sequence, depending on the experience and needs of the class.

Grammar: writer intention, reader response and creative imitation

The work of skilful and experienced children's authors, who know how to make worlds and engage readers, is one of the main resources we have for showing children what words can do. (Barrs.M, 2000:54).

Working with a fictional text over time provides an opportunity for children and teachers to think together about the effect a text has on them as readers, consider the way a writer has used language and possible reasons for the choices made. This will enable children to make connections between being a reader and being a writer, and equip them with a richer range of language choices to draw on and perhaps imitate in their own writing. Here is an example of Year 6 children in Brent, London, discussing the use of language in *The Wolf Wilder*, as suggested in the teaching sequence referred to in Chapter 4:

'I liked the very first sentence 'there was a dark and stormy girl,' that's a good way to start a book you can't really get a dark and stormy girl, it's saying she's brave and dangerous but you find out she's also kind.'

'I liked the way [the wolf] Grey was described 'the flick of her ears suggested she was invincible'. She sounds so strong.'

The opening to *The Outlaw Varjak Paw* by S.F. Said might be discussed in terms of what children visualise, or how it makes them feel:

It was winter in the city. The sun was sinking fast. Night was drawing in. Snow whipped down from the sky in icy flakes. It was too cold for snow to melt so it covered everything in white: the rooftops and drain pipes, the back streets and alleys. (S.F. Said, 2010:7).

Discussion might also focus on the effectiveness of a series of short sentences in building tension and creating drama. The verb choice might be noted, for example children could consider why the writer chose 'whipped' instead of 'fell' to describe the snow. This sort of discussion, which may include some use of relevant terminology (metalanguage), can support children with making their own language choices when writing (Myhill *et al.*, 2016; Reedy and Bearne, 2013).

Teaching approaches that help in developing an awareness of writer's use of language

Figure 6.2: Text marking, selecting memorable language

In Chapter 3 a broad range of creative teaching approaches were described in some depth. In summary, approaches which develop an awareness of language include: the teacher reading a text aloud and re-reading specific parts; booktalk; highlighting memorable language through text marking; making word and language collections; and performing the text through readers' theatre and choral poetry.

The key here is to work with the text and what it offers in terms of use of language rather than trying to shoehorn study of an aspect of grammar when it is not a particular feature, does not reflect the strength of a text and is not relevant to associated writing tasks. To do so would risk damaging both children's engagement with a powerful narrative, and the flow provided by a carefully constructed teaching sequence.

Chapter 7

Conclusion

In this Minibook I have aimed to provide guidance on how to approach planning with a whole text, including what to look for when choosing texts, the kinds of teaching approaches likely to be effective and how to go about constructing a coherent and engaging teaching sequence. This is further illustrated in the context of a teaching sequence in Chapter 5. Frequent concerns, such as covering a range of types of writing and making meaningful cross curricular links, have also been addressed.

Starting with a shorter text such as a picturebook, short story or narrative poem may be advisable if new to working in this way. Before embarking on planning with a novel you are less familiar with, it may be helpful to introduce it as part of your read aloud programme first of all, perhaps introducing one or two of the teaching approaches at key points in the story. If specific approaches, such as drama techniques, are unfamiliar it might be advisable to trial these, perhaps with a text you know well, before embarking on a full teaching sequence.

Schools moving towards a 'literacy through literature' programme might find it advisable to introduce one text per half term initially and plan staff meeting opportunities to discuss experiences and share ideas. Ultimately, decisions need to be taken about which books to focus on in each year group in order to ensure a good range and a balanced experience across the school as a whole.

Working creatively with carefully chosen literature can have dramatic impact on children's engagement and achievement. Active engagement in choosing rich texts and creating teaching sequences around them can be a satisfying, energising and potentially transformative experience for teachers too. One experienced head teacher, committed to a book based approach, comments:

'There is a real buzz about learning. Children throughout the school are mesmerised by their work in literacy based on the use of quality books. Not surprisingly, the result is that they, in turn, produce high quality work themselves.'

I hope this Minibook will encourage teachers, at all stages of their career, to develop their pedagogy and recognise the potential of a literacy curriculum with quality literature at its heart.

UKLA

References: Children's literature

Picture books KS1

Bartram, S. *Man on the Moon: a day in the life of Bob*, Templar Publishing, ISBN 978 184011491 1

Carle, E. *The Very Hungry Caterpillar*, Puffin, ISBN 978 0140569322

Carr, M. *Superbat*, Scholastic, ISBN 978 1407172828

Davies, B. *The Storm Whale*, Simon and Schuster, ISBN 978 1471115684

Gravett, E. *Tidy,* Two Hoots, ISBN 978 1447273981

Grey, M. *The Bad Bunnies Magic Show*, Simon and Schuster, ISBN 978 147115792

Grey, M. *Traction Man is Here!* Red Fox, ISBN 978 1862306400

Jeffers, O. *Lost and Found*, HarperCollins, ISBN 978 0007150366

Litchfield, D. *Grandad's Secret Giant*, Francis Lincoln, ISBN 978 1847808486

Sarah, L., Davies, B. (illus.) *On Sudden Hill*, Simon and Schuster, ISBN 978 1471119293

Turnbull, V. *Pandora*, Frances Lincoln, ISBN 978 1847807496

Vere, E. *Mr Big*, Puffin, ISBN 978 0141500607

Picture books KS2

Baker Smith, G. *FArTHER*, Templar Publishing, ISBN 978 1848771260

Browne, A. *Gorilla*, Walker Books, ISBN 978 1406352337

Browne, A. *The Tunnel*, Walker Books, ISBN 978 1406313291

Browne, A. *Zoo*, Red Fox, ISBN 978 0099219019

Davies, N. and Carlin, L. *The Promise*, Candlewick Press, ISBN 978 0763693039

Greder, A. *The Island*, Allen and Unwin, ISBN 978 1741752663

Hathorn, L. and Rogers,G. (illus.) *Way Home*, Andersen Press, ISBN 978 1842702321

Litchfield, D. *The Bear and the Piano*, Francis Lincoln, ISBN 978 1847807182

Milner, K. *My Name is not Refugee*, The Bucket List, ISBN 978 1911370062

Sanna, F. *The Journey*, Flying Eye Books, ISBN 978 1909263994

Tan, S. *The Arrival*, Hodder Children's Books, ISBN 978 0340969939

Wiesner, D. *Flotsam*, Andersen Press, ISBN 978 1849394499

Wiesner, D. *Tuesday*, Andersen Press, ISBN 978 1849394475

Zoboli, G. and Di Giorgio, M. (illus.) *Professional Crocodile*, Chronicle Books, ISBN 978 1452165066

Novels

Almond, D. *Skellig*, Hodder, ISBN: 978 0340944950

Almond, D. and McKean, D. (illus.) *The Savage*, Walker Books, ISBN 978 1406319859

Almond, D, McKean, D. (illus.) *The Savage* (graphic novel), Walker, ISBN 978 1406319859

Carroll, E. *Letters to the Lighthouse*, Faber and Faber, ISBN 978 0571327584

Doherty, B. *Streetchild*, HarperCollins, ISBN 978 0006740209

Doherty, B. *Treason*, Andersen Press, ISBN 978 1849391214

Dowd, S. *The London Eye Mystery*, Puffin, ISBN 978 0141376554

Durrant, S.E. *Little Bits of Sky*, Nosy Crow, ISBN 978 0857633996

Elphinstone, A. *Sky Song*, Simon and Schuster, ISBN 978 1471146077

Hughes, T. *The Iron Man*, Faber and Faber, ISBN 978 0571226122

Laird, E. *Welcome to Nowhere*, Macmillan, ISBN 978 1509840472

Leonard, M.G. *Beetle Boy*, Chicken House, ISBN 978 1910002704

Lewis, G. *Gorilla Dawn*, OUP, ISBN 978 0192739179

Lewis, G. *Skyhawk*, OUP, ISBN: 978 0192756237

Magorian, M. *Goodnight Mister Tom*, Puffin, ISBN 978 0141354804

Palacio, R.J. *Wonder*, Corgi, ISBN 978 0552565974

Paver, M. *Wolf Brother*, Orion, ISBN 978 1842551318

Reeve, P. and McIntyre, S. (illus.) *Pugs of the Frozen North*, OUP, ISBN 978 0192734921

Rundell, K. *The Wolf Wilder*, Bloomsbury, ISBN 978 1408854853

Rundell, K. *The Explorer*, Bloomsbury, ISBN 978 1408882191

Sachar, L *There's a Boy in the Girls' Bathroom*, Bloomsbury, ISBN 9 780747552574

Said, S.F. *Varjak Paw*, Random House, ISBN 9 780552548182

Said, S.F. *The Outlaw Varjak Paw*, David Fickling Books, ISBN 978 1849920469

Said, S.F. *Phoenix*, David Fickling Books, ISBN 978 0385618144

White, E.B. *Charlotte's Web*, Penguin, ISBN 9 780141317342

Traditional stories

McAllister, A. *A Year Full of Stories*, Frances Lincoln, ISBN 9 781847808592

Souhami, J. *The Leopard's Drum*, Frances Lincoln, ISBN 978 1845075064

Soundar, C. and Frané Lessac (illus.) *Pattan's Pumpkin*, Candlewick Press, ISBN 978 0763692742

See also collections by Hugh Lupton, Daniel Morden and Geraldine McCaughrean.

Non-fiction books

Adams, E. and Weston Lewis, J. *The Great Fire of London: Anniversary Edition of the Great Fire of 1666*, Wren and Rook, ISBN 978 0750298209

Benjamin, F. *Coming to England*, Macmillan, ISBN 978 1509835485

Davies, N. and Fisher, C. (illus.) *The Pond*, Graffeg Ltd, ISBN 978 1912050703

Grill, W. *Shackleton's Journey*, Flying Eye, ISBN 978 1909263109

Hooper, M. and Robertson, M. (illus.) *Ice trap! Shackleton's Incredible Expedition*, Frances Lincoln, ISBN 978 0711217447

Mandela, N., Van Wyck, C. and Bourna, P. (illus.) *Long Walk to Freedom*, Macmillan, ISBN 978 1447275541

Martin, M. *A River*, Templar, ISBN 978 1783704330

Poetry

Narrative poems

Agard, J. 'The Windrush Child' in Agard, J. and Nichols, G. *Under the Moon and Over the Sea*, Walker, ISBN 978-1406334487

Causley, C. 'What has happened to Lulu?' in *Collected Poems for Children*, Macmillan, ISBN 9 781447281023

Lear, E. and Beck, I. (illus.) *The Owl and the Pussycat*, Corgi, ISBN 9 780552528191

Noyes, A. and Keeping, C. (illus.) *The Highwayman*, OUP, ISBN 978 0192794420

Seraillier, I 'The Visitor' in McGough, R. (ed.) *100 Best Poems for Children*, Puffin, ISBN 9 780141310589

Poetry anthologies

Crebin, J. (ed.) *The Puffin Book of Fantastic First Poems*, Puffin, ISBN 978 0141308982

Duffy, C.A. (ed.) *101 Poems for Children*, Macmillan, ISBN 978 1447220268

McGough, R. (ed.) *100 Best Poems for Children*, Puffin, ISBN 9 780141310589

Film

Baldwin, J. *The Windmill Farmer*. Los Angeles: UCLA Animation Workshop. https://vimeo.com/12377177 (last accessed 1.5.2018).

Duriez, C. *Baboon on the Moon*. Bournemouth: Arts Institute https://vimeo.com/58445945 (last accessed 1.5.2018).

Disney, W. *Toy Story*, Pixar Animation Studios

S.F. Said's sci-fi adventure *Phoenix* https://www.youtube.com/watch?v=p5yQjwqDFXA (last accessed 1.5.2018).

Useful Links

For recommended books, films, poetry and related resources:

For a selection of teaching sequences see http://bit.ly/2BwP6wf .

University education departments sometimes have lists or curated collections such as this from UCL IoE http://bit.ly/28IUhgz .

For themed and age group selections, talk and activity ideas for EYFS, KS1 and Lower KS2 http://www.lovemybooks.co.uk/ .

For recommended books for KS2 http://www.guidingreaders.com/ .

The UKLA book award is a useful source of some of the best newly published books https://ukla.org/awards/ukla-book-award .

See also CLPE core books https://www.clpe.org.uk/corebooks .

The Literacy Shed has a wide selection of short films http://www.literacyshed.com/home.html .

National Gallery *Take One Picture* programme for narrative paintings and related resource packs for schools https://www.nationalgallery.org.uk/take-one-picture .

The Poetry Archive http://bit.ly/2G7pvK3 .

Poetryline http://bit.ly/2szwada .

References

Arizpe, E. and Styles, M. (2014) *Visual Journeys through Wordless Narratives*, London: Bloomsbury.

Arizpe, E. and Styles, M. (2015) *Children Reading Picture books: Interpreting Visual Texts*, Abingdon: Routledge.

Barrs, M. (2000) 'The Reader in the Writer' in *Reading*, UKRA 34:2, 54- 60.

Barrs, M. and Cork, V. (2001) *The Reader in the Writer*, London: CLPE.

Bearne, E. and Reedy, D. (2018) *Teaching Primary English: Subject knowledge and classroom practice*, Abingdon: Routledge.

Bunting, J., Nicholson, D., McGonigle, S. and Barrs, M. (2011) *BookPower: Literacy through Literature Year 6*, London: CLPE.

Chambers, A. (2011) *Children, Reading and Talk and the Reading Environment*, Stroud: Thimble Press.

Clark, C. (2013) *Children and Young People's Reading in 2012: Findings from the 2012 National Literacy Trust's Annual Survey*, http://bit.ly/2qEuTxs; (last accessed 1.5.2018).

Collins, F. M. (2014) pp 35- 52 in Cremin, T., Mottram, M., Collins, F. M., Powell, S. and Safford, K. (eds.) *Building Communities of Engaged Readers*, Abingdon: Routledge.

Cremin,T. (2009) *Teaching English Creatively*, Abingdon: Routledge.

Cremin, T., Mottram, M., Collins, F. M., Powell, S. and Safford, K. (eds.) (2014) *Building Communities of Engaged Readers*, Abingdon: Routledge.

DfE (2008) *Getting Going: generating, shaping and developing ideas in writing*, http://webarchive.nationalarchives.gov.uk/20121206151121/ https://www.education.gov.uk/publications/standard/English/Page1/ DCSF-00283-2008 (last accessed 1.5.2018).

DfE (2012) *What is the research evidence on writing?*, https://assets.publishing.service.gov.uk/government/uploads/system/ uploads/attachment_data/file/183399/DFE-RR238.pdf (last accessed 1.5.2018).

DfE (2013) *The National Curriculum in England*, http://bit.ly/2ESoKCU; (last accessed 1.5.2018).

DfE (2017) *Progress in International Reading Literacy Study (PIRLS) National Report for England*, http://bit.ly/2qEAVyE; (last accessed 1.5.2018).

DfES (2003) *Working in role useful classroom techniques in Speaking listening and learning working with children in key stages one and two*, http://dramaresource.com/wp-content/uploads/2017/08/Drama-Primary-National-Strategy.pdf; (last accessed 1.5.2018).

Evans,J. (2015) *Challenging and Controversial Picturebooks*, Abingdon: Routledge.

Gamble, N. (2013) *Exploring Children's Literature: Reading with pleasure and purpose*, London: Sage.

Grainger, T., Goouch, K. and Lambirth, A. (2005) 'Drama', in *Creativity and Writing: Developing voice and verve in the classroom*, Abingdon: Routledge.

Hardy, B. (1977) 'Narrative as a Primary Act of Mind' in Meek, M., Warlow, A. and Barton, G. (eds.) *The Cool Web*, London: The Bodley Head.

Kidd, D. C. and Costano, E. (2013) 'Reading literary fiction improves theory of mind', *Science*, 342(6156), 377–80.

Leland, C. H., Lewison, M. and Harste, J. C. (2018) *Teaching children's Literature - it's Critical*, New York: Routledge.

Maine, F. (2015) *Dialogic Readers: children talking and thinking together about visual texts*, Abingdon: Routledge.

Mallett, M. (2016) *A Guided Reader to Early Years and Primary English*, London: David Fulton.

Marsh, J. (2004) *Popular Culture, New Media and Digital Literacy in Early Childhood*, Abingdon: Routledge.

Martin, T. (2011) 'Readers making meaning: responding to narrative' in Goodwin, P. (ed.) *The Literate Classroom*, Abingdon: David Fulton.

McGonigle, S. (2002) 'Starting with Enthusiasm' in Barrs, M. and Pidgeon, S. (eds.) *Boys and Writing*, London: CLPE.

Meek, M. (1988) *How Texts Teach what Readers Learn*, Stroud: Thimble Press.

Moss, G. (2017) 'Assessment, Acountability and the Literacy Curriculum: reimagining the future in the light of the past'; *Literacy* 51:2, 56-64.

Myhill, D., Jones, S., Watson, A. and Lines, H. (2016) *Essential Primary Grammar*, Maidenhead: OUP.

Nikolajeva, M. (2013) 'Picturebooks and Emotional Literacy' in *The Reading Teacher* 67:4, 249-254.

OECD (2002) *Reading for Change Performance and Engagement across Countries, Results from PISA 2000*, **http://bit.ly/2HrPxuV**, (last accessed 1.5.2018).

O'Sullivan, O. and McGonigle, S. (2010) 'Transforming readers: teachers and children in the Centre for Literacy in Primary Education Power of Reading Project', *Literacy* 44:2.

Parry, B. and Hill Bulman, J. (2017) *Film Education, Literacy and Learning*, Leicester: UKLA.

Powell, S. (2014) 'Influencing children's attitudes, motivation and achievements as readers', in Cremin *et al.* (eds.) *Building Communities of Readers*, Abingdon: Routledge.

PNS (2003) National Archives, Speaking, Listening, learning, drama, key teaching points http://webarchive.nationalarchives.gov.uk/20110202170456/ https://nationalstrategies.standards.dcsf.gov.uk/node/88194?uc=force_uj , (last accessed 1.5.2018).

PIRLS findings (2011) http://oucea.education.ox.ac.uk/research/recent-research-projects/pirls/previous-pirls-findings/, (last accessed 1.5.2018).

Reedy, D. and Bearne, E. (2013) *Teaching Grammar Effectively in Primary Schools*, Leicester: UKLA.

Roche, M. (2015) *Developing Children's Critical Thinking through Picturebooks*, Abingdon: Routledge.

Rosen, M. (2018) *Poetry and Stories for Primary and Lower Secondary Schools*, London: Michael Rosen.

Roser, N., Martinez, M., Fuhrken, C. and McDonnold, K. (2007) 'Characters as Guides to Meaning' in *The Reading Teacher* 60:6.

Smith, K.T. (2014) *Teaching with Text Based Questions*, New York: Taylor and Francis.

Smith, V. (2016) 'Children's literature in the classroom and curriculum' in Wyse,D., Hayward, L. and Pandya, J. (eds.) *The Sage Handbook of Curriculum, Pedagogy and Assessment*, London: Sage.

Sullivan, A. and Brown, M. (2013) *Social Inequalities in Cognitive Scores at age 16: The role of reading*, London: Centre for Longitudinal Studies, UCL, http://bit.ly/2H6YE55, (last accessed 1.5.2018).

Tennent, W., Reedy, D., Hobsbaum, A. and Gamble, N. (2016) *Guiding Readers - Layers of Meaning*, London: UCL IOE Press.